HE WHO HAS EARS

Sister Thedra

ISBN: 978-1-7366487-9-7

CONTENTS

Mission Statement

Give the truth to the world. Let it be received where it will. Many will read the messages. Some will accept the truth, others will read through curiosity, a few will ridicule. Yet to all is the truth given, and to all remains the power of choice.

The hope of the world in these times is in spiritualizing all forms of activity---promoting understanding through love and service. These must be the watchwords if the world is to come into lasting peace. We are trying to influence a world that is going astray and could cause undreamed of suffering. We are trying to overcome the thought of materialists and to bring a spiritual outlook into the earthly life. We need the help of all on earth who can think in spiritual terms. The great battle to be fought now is between the spiritual and the material, between idealism and carnalism. You can help by spreading the word---we are asking that you help because the battle may be long and the victory far away.

Halls of Light is not allied with any sect, denomination, political entity, organization, neither endorses nor opposes any cause. There are no dues for membership. Halls of Light is self-supporting through its own voluntary contributions. Halls of Light has but one purpose: to help through encouragement and understanding...

To contact the publishers or to obtain copies of our other books, please contact us at email: goldtown11@gmail.com

Esu Jesus Sananda

This reproduction is from an actual photograph taken on June 1st, 1961, in Chichen Itza, Yucatan, by one of thirty archaeologists working in the area at the time. Sananda appeared in visible, tangible body and permitted His photograph to be taken.

Sananda's Appearance

Be ye as one which hast heard Mine Voice and responded unto it - for I speak that ye hear, and I say that which is wise and prudent.

Let it be known that I, the Lord thy God hast spoken and bear ye witness of Me, for I have made manifest Mineself that ye might know Me - and for this was these manifestations made.

I say I have made Mineself manifest that ye might see Me with thine mortal eyes; that ye might bear witness of Me. Yet thine companions saw and believed not; neither did they hear, for they were selfish and unprepared - yet did I deny them?

I say; I came that they which would might see and hear. I went and came again unto Mine own. So be it that I have found; I have given unto the found that they which know not might KNOW; that they might come to know as thou knowest.

Yet, how many hast turned from Me and persecuted thee for Mine Word. It is said, "Woe unto them which persecute Mine servants." Is it not the law which they set into motion?

Yea, Mine beloved, I say they bring about their own downfall. So be it that I am a compassionate one, and I would that they know what they do.

So be it they shall learn well their lessons. So let it be, for this is the mercy of God, the One which hast sent me.

So be it I AM the wayshower, the Lord thy God.

I AM Sananda

"Recorded by Sister Thedra"

To you, the reader of "The Sibors Portions, these words are addressed that you may know something about the one who has been and is the Channel thru whom these writings have been received. In the "Portions" or "Holy Scripts", the messages are concluded by the words, "Recorded by Sister Thedra of the Emerald Cross" or "Recorded by Sister Thedra of the School of the Seven Rays". It should be self-evident that these titles could not and should not be used without proper authority.

To answer these and other questions that have been asked, we of The Association Sananda & Sanat Kumara, herein present a brief biographical sketch of Sister Thedra, that you might know something of the background of this remarkable woman; that you might come to know that it is only by the most intensive and extensive preparation, training, obedience, dedication and discipline, that one may become worthy to be used by such exalted Beings as Sananda. (Jesus the Christ), Sanat Kumara and other great Sibors and Teachers of the Higher Realms, to channel messages of Truth, Love and Hope to those who are "Seekers of Truth", and who hunger for "The Bread and Water of Life".

What is the background of Sister Thedra? What experiences did she need to go thru in order to become ready to be used as a Channel? What are her qualifications and special Spiritual Gifts? What qualities of mind and character are required in order that one may ascend to that high position of responsibility that merits the recognition by our Blessed Lord God Sananda, as, "Mine Beloved"; Mine Beloved Priestess, whom I have authorized to speak in Mine Name?"

Sister Thedra

The name 'Thedra" was given to her by the Lord God Sananda, at the beginning of her ministry. At an early age Sister Thedra manifested unusual ability to foresee events and facts by keen spiritual insight, or by what is now recognized as "Extra sensory perception". She was born in the year 1900. Educational facilities were limited in those days in her area, thus her education was somewhat limited. She went thru many trials, frustrations and illnesses too numerous to mention; but it may be truly said that three of these illnesses literally took her thru the portals of death. It was only by the power of her indomitable will, that she survived such severe illnesses as spiral meningitis, lymphatic cancer, partial paralysis, and a terrible automobile accident.

To elaborate somewhat on her third serious illness: In 1950 Sister Thedra was in an automobile accident, and was so severely injured that she was hospitalized and in a cast for 9 months, and was told by her doctors that she could never walk again - in fact they secretly admitted that they did not expect her to survive. She was little more than a skeleton when the cast was finally removed, and she lay totally helpless, and could not move or help herself, and had to be carried and cared for like a baby. The day that the doctors removed the cast, they also discontinued all drug treatments. On this same day her earthly papa died - but they hesitated to tell her. The next morning when her doctor asked her: "Do I look like the bearer of news?" She answered, "Yes I know - last night I walked with Papa part way, looking down on the earth. As we went, hand in hand, he turned to me saying, 'Honey you cannot go further, you must go back'". The doctor understood, for he had had a similar experience during the war.

During her long months of agony in the cast, Sister Thedra had continual communication with Jesus, and was comforted by His assurances that He would be "with her all the way". She came to the inner knowledge that she was actually and literally "In the palm of The Father's hand". It took nearly a year of the most determined, agonizing effort, which anyone of less determination would have given up as impossible, that this blessed one was able to finally get from her walker and wheel chair, on to crutches - for she had developed severe arthritis in her hips and hands. By 1952 she was being subjected to treatments for lymphatic cancer in a clinic a great distance from her home. It was a torturous ordeal to prepare for the long trip (she was still struggling with her crutches) to the clinic for a series of treatments, even though her mother accompanied and assisted her.

When she was notified that it was time for another series of treatments, her very inner being rebelled - she felt that "There must be a better way". From the depths of her soul she cried out to The Father: "Father Thy Will be done - if it is Thy Will heal me - if not I am ready to go". The One known to her then as Jesus appeared at her side and laid His hand on her throat, and she was instantly healed of the cancer. He said that He would restore her to usefulness. She could have her complete healing now, or "Wait for the greater part". She replied at once: "I will wait for the greater part". She asked what she could do to repay such a debt - He answered, "Go feed My sheep - I will give you the Food and the Water".

Thru the powerful help of Sananda and her unseen Teachers, Thedra, by steel will and determination continued to improve, and was restored to usefulness, although she still had to struggle with her crippled body, and was never without pain. She was in continual communication with Sananda (then known to her as Jesus), and other great Teachers and

4

Sibors, from whom she received revelations, prophecies and Words of Living Truth, which she gave forth to the ever-increasing numbers who sought her counsel. During this time the One Who has been known for centuries as Jesus revealed Himself to her in person, and gave her His New Name - Sananda, and instructed her to give it forth to all mankind.

The story of how Sister Thedra carried out His instructions; of how she carried on in the face of humiliations, tribulations and Judas type betrayals, when the forces of darkness seemed to be striving to disrupt and stop her work at any cost; of how, at the most crucial point of this trying time, Sananda's Aides stepped in and whisked her away to a place of safety - never to return to her home again - would fill a volume! Someday, when the time is right, the full story of Sister Thedra's life will be told, and it will be a thrilling story indeed!

After a few months in her "place of safety", Sister Thedra was instructed by Sananda to go to the region of Peru & Bolivia, in the high Andes mountains near Lake Titicaca. She was to go "without purse or script", and with only that which she could carry in her hand. The following five years - from 1955 to 1961 – were spent under conditions of almost unbearable hardships, sacrifices, humiliations, privations, tribulations and severe discipline. She was instructed to get right down to bedrock, and live with and as the natives; to observe their hard ships, filth, squalor and unbelievable poverty.

Thus she learned first-hand the lowly state in which people are fated to live very little better than animals. During this period of training and observation of the traits and habits of native existence, Sister Thedra learned the true meaning of Divine Love for these unfortunate people, who were experiencing the penalty meted out by "higher laws" to those who, in times past have betrayed their trust, and refused God's Grace when it was offered them; who chose the way of darkness. These were years of training her for the heavy responsibilities which, unknown to her, were to be placed upon her shoulders in succeeding years. Few there are who could have faced the disappointments, humiliation and frustration she experienced when her inspired writings, received from Sananda and other Teachers and Sibors of the Higher Realms, were sent back to the United States at great personal sacrifice, often with postage taken from her very meager food money, only to be received with ridicule and scorn.

Many hundreds of pages of word-for-word recordings of the communications from these High Spiritual Beings were kept, and are to be found in the Holy Scripts which follow this "Portion". Among the great Beings Who revealed Themself and communicated with Sister Thedra during these years, was the great Angel Moroni, who foretold several years in advance, how He would arrange for a certain young man and young woman in the United States to meet and marry. Moroni gave Sister Thedra many revelations and instructions which were to be delivered to the baby boy who would be born to this couple. This baby boy was to be the embodiment of Moroni, and was to be unlike any other child, in that he would be born with his memory - with his mind fully awake. The story of how, later, after Sister Thedra had returned to the States in 1961, the father and mother to be, as was foretold by Moroni, met and were married; and how the baby boy was born on the 24th of August 1963, is just one convincing proof of the accuracy and truth of the words "Recorded by Sister Thedra".

The Temple teachings contain many revelations and instructions which were given by Moroni to the parents during the pregnancy. Intimate details are revealed regarding this remarkable child, and the part he is to play in history, and his destiny as a world leader. He will hold the

6

fullness of the Melchezedek Priesthood, and will come in the office of one of the highest Angels. How His coming is destined to affect every person, Church, Nation and people of the Earth, is only part of the mighty truths and disclosures of the "Work of The Father" - "The great and marvelous news", which have been "Recorded by Sister Thedra" - the humble and completely dedicated servant of God, who has been authorized by Sananda to "speak in His Name".

At the time Sister Thedra made her covenant with The Father that she would do His Will, she dedicated her life and will completely to the great assignment given to her by Sananda: "Go feed My Sheep". She learned to have absolute faith and confidence in His guidance and protection. She yielded her will completely to The Father, that His Will might be done "In her, thru her, by her and for her". She learned to live one day at a time, accepting all the trials and experiences of that day as part of her training for "The Greater Part". She sought to accept and "drain her cup of experience to the very dregs". Her sojourn in the High Andes was part of that training. She fully expected to spend the remainder of her life in the flesh in that region.

It was eventually revealed to her that she would be sent back to her native land to carry out a mission that would be revealed to her at the proper time. She humbly accepted this assignment. At the expiration of five years, she was told that great responsibility would be placed upon her shoulders. She was to return to her native land and disseminate the Teachings of "The School of the Seven Rays" that she had and would continue to receive. She was sent back to California in 1961, not knowing how nor where she was to go or do. She relied on day-to-day instructions and guidance by her Teachers in the Higher Realms. She lived in southern California for nearly a year, receiving daily instructions and revelations, which she shared with those who sought her counseling.

In 1962 Sister Thedra was instructed by Sananda to go to Mt. Shasta, California to establish "His Work". She followed His instructions, and after coming to Mt. Shasta she again went thru many almost unbelievable trials, testings and betrayals at the hands of those who professed to be her friends who had volunteered to assist her in the work. Thru all of these trials, privations and disappointments, her steel will never wavered. She had complete faith in the continual assurance of Sananda that He knew exactly what was going on, and He "would be with her all the way". The instructions from both Sananda and Sanat Kumara for setting up the "Altar", "Temple" and "Gate House" are contained in the "Holy Scripts" that follow this "Portion".

After several moves here in Mt. Shasta, the present property was acquired in a most wonderful manner in 1965. The two Great Ascended Beings -Sananda and Sanat Kumara, Who supervised the acquiring of the property, gave instructions that the Work should bear Their Names. The Work consists of both exoteric and esoteric aspects. The "Gate House" is the exoteric headquarters of the "Association Sananda & Sanat Kumara". The esoteric aspect is 'The Temple of Sananda & Sanat Kumara". Sister Thedra is the "Custodian of the Gate House" and "Priestess in the Temple". She has accepted the great responsibility of this assignment. She disclaims any special wisdom or other qualities that have led to the successful establishment of the Gate House, and the wonderful activity carried on herein, and gives full credit to Sananda, Sanat Kumara and the Great and Mighty Council, Who have not only provided the place and facilities; They are also providing the opportunity to sincere students to become "Associates" in this great Work of service to mankind.

The activities of the Gate House are supported solely by the contributions of our associates. The complete story of the most remarkable career of Sister Thedra will become known in time to come.

A.S.S.K. Inc.
P.O. Box 35
Mt. Shasta Ca. 96067

"LET NOT YOUR HEARTS BE TROUBLED"

From Hilarion…Again as the MASTER told us: "Let not your hearts be troubled"…Surely the "Shaking" has started. Do not be alarmed. Proceed in your "orderly way" with the work you have been given., even as We, in these periods of stress and strain.

"Everything is in its place and progressing according to Divine Plan, and order…ALL IS WELL…I too, saw darkly as through a screen, but now I see the perspective in the "Divine Plan", so shall you, be faithful, be strong, and be of good courage. If you pause to reflect that in ages past there was not the protection of the people that you now have. There was not the way you have under the "New Covenant" of LOVE and MERCY…deep and wide. In this point of space and time all creation knows the deepest LOVE" and the widest Mercy and opportunity ever given as the consciousness of mankind in knowledge and wisdom and understanding.

I have told you there must be the "SHAKING" in order that the old may cease to exist and the new order shall unfold with it's "golden Light encompassing all life. Today you are uncomfortable, Beloved Friends, because the Karma of the past has come to life before your very eyes making you aware of the "spiritual" wickedness in high places. Manipulations of greed and aggrandizement on material planes of seeking have made your monies of little worth in this day. Fear of the unknown and fear of the future are shaking many, many people. Accidents and catastrophes are common all across the world, even as it was foretold by many seers and prophets in the past.

This is only, and I say with all LOVE, only the beginning of sorrows, I say again "be practical" use your common sense and your LOVE, and deal with all situations on your earth plane in the "Light of LOVE"...Call into action all your spiritual energies and your knowledge of how to change situations. Use your knowledge of "precipitation and "alchemy" to acquire that which is needed to meet the situations...Most important of all, see the "DIVINE" in each and every person...and HIS PLAN in all EVENTS. For the KNOWING ONES will use what they KNOW.

There is NO reason for "FEAR or DISMAY. Group activities are most important in these times, for in numbers, there is strength. In putting the "LIGHTS" together there is more knowledge and more wisdom and a greater understanding...ALL MUST STRENGTHEN EACH OTHER AND MAINTAIN THE HIGHER LEVEL OF FAITH IN THESE DIFFICULT TIMES. There must be TRUE COMMUNION in LIGHT, and an UNDERSTANDING for ALL these associated together. In this way the burden is not too heavy for any one to bear...for there are others to lend a hand. Each individual must grow and expand in the LIGHT, becoming ever a "BRIGHTER BEACON". That each individual seek for himself or herself, that his ears and eyes may be opened to "DIVINE GUIDANCE" from on HIGH. There are thousands coming into your atmosphere now, so there shall be adequate help given all those who need help from the "Spiritual realms". I would like to say, that if you could see the "intense LOVE" that surrounds you and all children of Light. The LIGHT Bodies of those who are in their places NOW, to minister and give aid...All are working to correct the "imbalances" in these days of judging the nations...the new "covenant is your aid else all mankind would have perished long ago...as did those in generations past.

Small wonder that the grossness of material greed and deception cannot exist with the "fine high vibratory" forces of the uplifting LOVE now present at the beginning of the "New Dawn". Be steadfast children…fight the good fight…and take all precautions dictated by common sense and "welcome all strangers lest ye turn away the "HOLY ONES" whose help you need at this time…Be very discerning of all who come your way. The energies are present in which you can precipitate all things…Work with the Precipitating forces of the "Energy Rays", and "DIVINE LOVE" and know that all is well. Results of the "SHAKING" will be going on daily now, so DO STAND IN THE LIGHT OF YOUR DIVINITY, WEARING THE ARMOR OF GOD, AS YOUR POLARITY SHIELD OF PROTECTION. Be stable, be ready. Be an EXAMPLE in POSITIVE-NESS every moment that's left in this Great Cosmic Plan.

OUR LOVE IS BEAMED TO ALL.

YOUR MENTOR, FROM SATURN OF ASHTAR COMMAND.
From the Gateway

"COMMUNICATION HAS AGAIN BEEN ESTABLISHED"

Beloved of Mine Being: I speak unto thee this day as thine Older Brother, which hast seen and watched the world of men seethe within the cauldron of their own firing. I say: They have been unto themself their own tormentors; they have gone forth from the realm of Light as one perfect, and they have taken unto themself the daughters of men, that they might bring forth a generation of vipers - and that they might set themself up as creators of the very thing which now torments them.

For I say unto thee: They, the ones which came into physical flesh for the purpose of lifting them up, have become drunken on the "new wine" and they have forgotten their origin - their mission. They have wandered blindly for the most part, knowing not that they have forfeited their inheritance for a time. Yet it is now come when the Great and Mighty Host hast drawn nigh, and the means of communication hast again been established, between the Angelic Host; these are the Ones which have not walked the Earth in forms of flesh - physical bodies.

While We, the Grand Master (Sananda) and Myself, have taken upon Ourself the form of flesh, and the flesh might be purified, sanctified, and lifted up.

I say that: The elements of the Earth shall be purified, sanctified and made new, as in the beginning, when it was nothing but pure fire - White Fire! - the Substance from which it was created. I say: It was clean! pure! and undefiled – now it shall again be purified, and the blessed Virgo and Her Consort, shall be justified for taking upon

13

Themself such a preponderous task, as ensouling within the body of Earth. While it is now time that We, the Hierarchy, come unto Her assistance, that She too be unbound; I tell thee of a surety: Thou too hast a part in Her deliverance - ye too shall be mindful of Her. And there is a Mighty Service which all might render unto Her, for She cries out in Her birth pains - for She too suffers mighty, even as thine own body, for She carries the Greater burden - that of laggards and their creation!

Listen unto Me, Mine Beloved Ones, and take these Mine Words unto thine heart: The Earth hast been unto thee thine Benefactor and thine home, thine comforter - and ye have not been unto Her a 'thoughtful guest' - thou hast accepted Her Love, hospitality, and protection, comfort, beauty, without thought! I say unto thee: The pity of it! Look! See! that which She hast afforded thee, and take account of what thou hast given in return. I say unto thee: Listen unto Me - take ye account of what thou hast given in return!! Be ye thoughtful of thine Benefactors, and They shall remember thee in the time of stress - so be ye mindful of Them in the time of plenty.

I AM thine Older Brother, Sanat Kumara 3
Recorded by Sister Thedra of the Emerald Cross

BE READY!

I Am The Lord Thy God, thou shalt have no other Gods before Me. I Am The One and The All. I Am Love as I Am Wisdom and I do issue forth The Truth and The Law. And I say no man is exempt from The Law. I say all things of God must operate under and within The Law.

At this moment in your time there are many moving across the face of the planet Earth who speak of Earth changes, cataclysmic events that will alter the path of mankind.

Many are reacting to this information with fear. Many refuse to listen and I see them with their fingers in their ears. "Perhaps it will all go away if I don't hear it" they say. And there are those who obstinately scream liar at My messengers. And there are those who are lazy, they sleep today intending to "wake up" tomorrow.

I Am The Lord Thy God. My word to thee this day is "the night of the sleeper is swift coming to a close" -- comes the dawn and I say the dawn approaches and no thing shall hold it back. I say too that for many their awakening shall be rude indeed.

And you say what if there is no great shaking, what if the seas remain calm? How do I know this will come to pass?

I The Lord Thy God say what if there was no great shaking, what if the seas remained calm? What if the night remained? And the sleeper slept on? What if you had prepared yourself, lifted yourself, cleansed yourself. What if - you had come to learn to live in harmony with man and nature. What if you had learned to Love in the way of The Angels. What if you had done all that and no earthquake jarred your footing.

15

Because of My warnings if you had raised yourself up and had earned your wings, if because of your right behavior you had caused the Earth to move into the new dawn smoothly and without pain would you then feel you had wasted your effort? O Man you must "think" everything out so carefully - then think about My words to thee this day.

I say the "Dawn" cometh and no thing shall hold it back. I say be ready! Be the very best you that you can be at every given moment. Do not chastise yourself when you fall short and waste your energy but rather use that energy to get back "up" there - quickly! Raise yourself up to your optimum and I The Lord will say well done! I say the Hand of God can whisk you from your moorings on Earth in a flash. Be Ready!

Received Oct. 24, 1984 by Kai King
P.O. Box 3436
Gardena, CA 90247

"WE SHALL INCREASE THE ENERGIES TO OUR LIGHT WORKERS"

Good afternoon ladies and gentlemen. I am Monka to speak this hour. It is with a measure of joy that I express my gratitude that I might be able to communicate first-hand with some of you. Dear ones, as you look about your skies this day you see great beauty. As you look about Earth at this season you see the changing colors, the brilliance, the glory of your seasons of Earth. Know that this splendid display has of its purpose. For is it not a great show before you have your winter's sleep when all is the softness, the gentleness of the white, the Total of all the colors that have so beautifully danced about your Earth this fall? Yea, they are all gathered but shortly ye shall be blanketed in the beautiful white, your color of purity, your color of holiness. I would say to you dear ones the upcoming seasons are indeed ones that should be used each hour that you are upon Earth to raise your vibratory rate and to become more and more in tune with your Creator, the Divine Force, that One known to you as the Father-Mother God.

Currently aboard our ships there is an air of great solemnity for "yes" man has chosen to continue his ways and the efforts of the workers of Light upon the planet and our efforts here seem to have modified his direction minimally. We currently are shifting all of our efforts to the finalization plans for evacuations and lift-offs. We shall, in the upcoming days, increase the energies to our Light workers and to all Light workers. We shall be working with each one of you individually and closely. This is to raise your vibrational rate that you might be easily lifted up in the event this is necessary, or I should say, when this is necessary. Commander Andromeda Rex has spoken earlier and I would not repeat his instructions at this time for I am sure they too will be shared with you. I would but add my voice to say welcome to those of you with whom I have not had the opportunity to speak before. And to those of you with whom I have spoken I send my warmest affection, I say thank you for all of your efforts on behalf of all of the ones of Earth. And all of us here send our gratitude for allowing us to work with you and through you. Watch for us dear ones. Watch the skies. You shall see the shuttles as they play about your skies. Watch. Each one of you in your own way shall receive your confirmation, your verification of our existence. May the blessings and love of the Radiant One abide with each of you as you go forth. I am your brother in space signing off at this hour. Vassau, Vassau

Received thru Tuieta of the Golden Cross
Pt. Wayne, Indiana

ATTITUDE

You are Mine - and all that you are is of Me and by Me. All that you are I own. Yet Beloved there is one part and portion that is yours and yours alone. That part and portion called attitude -- Attitude -- What is it? It is of you - by you. It is not the test that is given that is of the greatest importance but rather the ATTITUDE of that one being tested.

Do you walk into a job ready to "do your part" - grumbling? Do you do your work with a heavy heart? When your trials are presented to you do you look for the little rays of light? Or do you see only the dark - therefore seeing nothing.

Beloved I say you cannot and you do not understand My Way. Judge ye not My Work - Mine Own and Mysterious Plan. What may seem obvious to you may not be My Truth.

When I call you are you willing to give up your truth and become One with All that is Mine? Can you let go of preconceived ideas - opinions. I say opinions are the rock in the darkness that will trip thee up.

Ask yourself - truthfully - when you say - Father Thy Will be done, in me, through me, by me and for me - do you secretly add - my way?

Child it is not always completing the "run" that is the greater part of the test - rather the ATTITUDE accompanying the experience. Can you perform without judging the work - or those you are "working out" with? Can you do even the most monumental or the most mediocre test with equal zeal? Can you get in there and do the really dirty jobs with bare hands? Can you be the healer - the communicator - the receiver? Can you also be the garbage collector and the one who would suck the venom from a brothers wound - in joy? Can you endure boredom as well as the excitement of your quest? Will you scrub your brothers back? - and if he throws dirty water in your face and denies in words of ugliness your worth - will you still serve him - thus serving me?

I ask of thee a gift this day. I ask you to give "up" to Me your attitude as well as your opinions.

<u>I want My Pure Babies Back!</u> I want My Babies <u>Home</u> --- unencumbered – unburdened – free as they went out from Me. Know that when you "fall down" My Love for you is not diminished for my Own Hand will pick you up and dust you off- And Child this message is a "dusting off". Now go about My Work - in My Way Trust Me to Know the Way. You Are Mine and <u>all</u> that you are is of Me and by ME. All that you are <u>I</u> <u>own</u>!

So do not hide a little piece from Me? Do I not know all -- See <u>All</u>. Stop your grumblings -- I say you know not the fullness of Me -- The extent of My Love - You know the smallest portion of My Power. You see a microcosm and call it Me -- Yes even the smallest part is <u>Me</u> - but I Am The Greater Part and your eye is not clear enough – yet – to know the Truth of Me. So Beloved <u>let Me See</u> for you. Trust Me to know what will be the greatest Nourishment for your complete and <u>total health</u>

Father

"THEY SHALL BE KNOWN AS THE TRAIL-BLAZERS"

Beloved Ones: While I am thy Sibor, thine Older Brother, I am prepared to give unto thee this Word - and it is for the good of all; so let them partake of this portion which I now give unto thee - for this do I give it unto thee, that ye might record it for them. While it is not given unto all to hear that which I say, it is given unto thee to have ears which hear that which I say - it is indeed a great gift for which thou hast prepared thyself.

Now let it be given unto them thusly: The time is come when the ones which have come into the world of flesh, for the purpose of mentoring or being unto thee the ears, the eyes, the feet, the parts which function from the Higher Level; these shall become known unto thee as the "Trail-blazers"- they have gone before thee knowing that theirs was a part which brought no reward from man - yet for the greater part, only suffering and persecution. While the unknowing ones thought themself wise - they jeered and taunted, and for that matter made foolish sayings unto and about them - these "Trail blazers", yet it is now come when ye shall come to know that they knew of which they spoke. Yet I say: Ye shall be mindful of them, and of thine own foolishness, far it shall rebound back to confront thee, and ye shall be as ones afronted with thine foolish sayings, for they shall come before thee to taunt thee.

Let thine lips be swift to retract them, and make restitution unto them which thou hast persecuted - be ye swift to ask of them forgiveness; lend a hand when possible to assist in this the day of learning - the day of enlightenment. Be ye swift to assist in the deliverance from bondage and darkness. I say: Ye shall first be enlightened, then ye shall know. It is said: First seek ye the Light and it shall not be denied thee.

21

Now it shall be said that the "Trail-blazers" have gone before thee as the "Spearmen", that the way be made clear before thee - and these are the ones strong of character, and filled with the Water of Spirit - the Water that quenches the thirst of them which doth hunger for Light, Truth and Justice. I say: These are Mine "Spearmen", for the seed of the new day which now dawns in the East - I say it dawns in the East. Be ye up and about the Word of the "New Day" - sleep not while it is dawning, for all nature cries out: "Awaken! Awaken! Look! See!"

Behold! and rejoice, for the new day breaks forth with a glad shout: Arise! come ye forth from out the pit - let thine heart be swift to rejoice! for I am come that ye awaken! Be ye blest this day.

I AM Sanat Kumara 3
Recorded by Sister Thedra

THE HOUR GLASS HAS RUN - MICHAEL

Hear ye mine word. Hear ye. It is Michael that does speak from out of the Universal, the Total. It is Michael that does speak. Hear ye mine word. As ye do hear so shall ye be as ones warned and so shall ye be as ones told. It is that the hourglass has run and the bowl is empty and man is at the end of the cycle. It is that he shall not be as one to dwell upon this time for this is the time of nothingness for all has been counted and all wait for that which shall be. For it shall be and ye ones who would recognize it shall be as the ones the wiser.

Now it is that the pestilence shall descend across the lands and ones shall then rise up from the sea and they shall be as ones unclean and they shall be as ones hungry. It is that I shall unsheath mine sword and the ones from the sea shall be slewn and the pestilence shall be stopped for I shall sweep across the lands and I shall sweep all that is unclean, that is unfit from the lands and from the sea. It shall be. Then it shall be that the Earth shall feel of the mighty rumble and it shall quake and groan. I say it shall quake and it shall groan and the lands shall be no more for they shall change and they shall go under to that place of rest. So be it as is given. It is that ones shall cling unto the lands and they shall be taken under that they shall be as ones to sleep with the lands that they do cling. It is that the mountain tops shall be as the islands and they shall be as the places that ones shall gather waiting - waiting - waiting.

I say ones shall wait and they shall moan and weep at what is about them and they shall be as ones sorrowful for their wrong doing and they shall be as ones to see of that which they have done and that which they ought to have done and they shall wecp. But they shall be as ones to watch and they shall be as ones to see for that is their lot and pity be for

23

them. It is that the lands shall alter and the lands shall change and ones shall not recognize that which is happening. Those that do hear of the still small whisper shall know and to them shall <u>all</u> the answers be given for they shall be as the ones that have been guided and they shall be as the ones who did profit from their lot and they shall be as the ones to see and to know: Now they shall try to give comfort to the lost ones and they shall try to speak, to tell, but they shall be as ones that do talk with the stones for they will not be heard for ones that do try to give to them the comfort shall be as ones that do call into the wind for naught shall go from them that is not received by the other. So be it as is given. So be it. Now it is that the hour approaches when all this shall be. Be ye as ones ready. Be ye as ones ready for all that shall come to thee. Now know ye that which ye have sent forth so shall it come to thee but in the final hour - the hour of the nothingness - so shall naught move but each shall stay as it is for that is the close of one that the next shall begin. Know ye that as the cycle does close so shall the next begin. So shall it begin. Now ye ones who have heard of the still small voice and ye ones who have practiced of that which ye have been given, ye shall be as ones to see and ye shall be as ones to balance that which is about you and you shall be of the balance. I say ye shall be of the balance. It is that ye shall be given that which is new and ye shall be adorned with thine jewels that are of thy station and ye shall behold as the heavens do open to receive thee. It will be that ye shall be as ones that shall commune within the heavens and the earth for they shall be as one. I am Michael that has spoken. Hear ye mine word and be ye as one to profit from the receiving.

Selah

Om ni di eno

Recorded by Tuieta

24

CAPTAIN ZOA, ASHTAR COMMAND

In 1970 we were informed:

"We are doing all we can from our position outside the earth to facilitate the work now being put into practice. You will appreciate we are not allowed to intervene by Karmic Law, and, desperate as the situation has become, we must abide by that Law of noninterference, for we have to bow to the Cosmic Laws laid down by our Creator. Nevertheless, the planet shall be saved from destruction if certain Powers decide on negative action. Their weapons shall be rendered powerless at the vital moment, and before that moment occurs, certain drastic changes will have taken place.

Changes MUST take place in accordance with Natural and Cosmic Laws set in motion long before mankind existed upon the earth. So fear not, Brothers and Sisters of the Light.

Life is changing all the time…all planets, suns, solar systems, universes are either developing or passing away. This is LIFE!"

When we find we are able to speak to people, one of our tasks will be to make sure they grasp that whatever happens the world is not to be destroyed - only changed <u>or reborn</u>!

COSMIC OPERATION COUNTERACTION

There is a FUNDAMENTAL CHANGE to come.

We do not know when this will occur but it is probable that within the next five years conditions on this planet will have altered beyond all recognition. We are not necessarily referring to geophysical changes, although they will be taking place as time goes on, but to social, economic and other dramatic changes in our way of living, our newly-found values and our attitude of mind and heart.

The rebirth of the Earth is inextricably interwoven with the rebirth of mankind as the planet moves from the Third to the Fourth Dimensional Frequency Scale. This is how one eminent New Age scientist describes this operation:

"The genetics of man are to function on a higher wavelength of LIGHT. In order to accomplish this the Brotherhood of LIGHT is accelerating the entire system of human biorhythms to enter a less dense spectrum of MATTER-ENERGY. "

This statement confirms information given to this and other Light Centres that we have begun the evolutionary movement back from DENSE MATTER to LIGHT... THE SOURCE OF ALL LIFE! or GOD!

THE ETERNAL SPIRALS

We should perhaps explain for the benefit of our new readers that in accordance with recurring Cosmic Laws we come down from the Higher Dimensions on an involutionary wave into dense Matter. Having reached the halfway mark on a Spiral we are now beginning to move UPWARDS on the evolutionary wave which takes us onto the next Level. We have touched rock-bottom in this Dimension and NOW can only move UPWARDS!

As a consequence we are facing NOW the most critical and turbulent period for mankind leading up to the MOMENT OF TRANSFORMATION...

THE FREQUENCY CHANGES

"The whole of creation is but ENERGY, manifesting in various ways. At its most dense state it forms the Physical Worlds of the Universe. At its highest Vibration, its highest Frequency Point, it is THAT WHICH YOU CALL 'GOD'. You distinguish God from the Physical! ALL PLANES OR STATES OF BEING are but different stages of the MANIFESTATION OF LIGHT - of the ONE ENERGY, OF ALL-BEING...WHICH IS GOD.

As you spread THE LIGHT VIBRATIONS throughout this Planet... it is NOT DOOMED! It is destined to be born again."

"Do not fear the frequency changes. Through them shall you be changed in body, mind and soul. Welcome the changes; they are vital to your own destiny and the rapid CHANGE TO COME. We implore you to be POSITIVE NOW. NOW is the TIME TO BE POSITIVE! Let the NEGATIVE go! There is no place for the Negative now, only room for the ETERNAL LOVE which is beyond the comprehension of mortal man."

ONTOLOGICAL PRELUDE

We offer you confirmation from a telepathic communication through the voice of Louise Morse of the U.S.A., a Channel of the Holy Spirit:

"You shall find that there will be a great change of vibrations around your earth. You shall become more and more sensitive. You shall find that in the years coming there will be an intensification that will raise your consciousness until the revitalizing of the cells of

27

your body shall transform. As you become used to the swiftly changing vibrations, entering into a new frequency, as it were, you shall be living in a new element, in the Fourth Dimension - that paradise state around your earth. You shall be changed in the twinkling of an eye* as the transmutation takes place. You are gradually changing and there shall be finally the Moment of changing over completely into the New Dimension. This shall be rapid."

The New Testament predictions fall into place when we interpret them anew. What we are beginning to witness is a reversal of the earth's present condition.

The earth is a unique planet in that it has been involved in a great rebellion (Revelation 12:7-9). As this rebellion is brought under control and as we cleanse ourselves and raise our vibrations through a loving, compassionate regard for others, prayer and meditation, so we become ready for 'this quantum leap' into a NEW ORDER, a new series of Evolutionary Patterns. We have to bring all our bodies into alignment so that we can live in harmony with ourselves and others. We are to be re-united with spiritual beings on other planets.

However, if we are not attuned to the Higher Frequency by the time the ENERGY PEAK is reached** we shall not be allowed to remain on the planet. At the time of composing this letter it would be true to say we are all being graded NOW. The Brothers do not make mistakes and everyone will be in their rightful place at the MOMENT OF CHANGE.

*I Cor. 15:51,52
**II Peter:3:10-12

AXMINSTER LIGHT CENTER

"Veronica Cote"

66 Willhayes Park, North Street,

AXMINSTER, DEVON,

ENGLAND. ÉX19 5QW

PREPARED TO MOVE ON A MOMENT'S NOTICE

Sori Sori - There is but little time that is left for the work that is to be done - and it is now time that there be ones alert and prepared to move on a moment's notice - for I say I have called thee out of thine bed to give them this word - it is for the good of all that I speak unto thee this hour (1:25 A.M.) Now the time grows shorter and ye are yet not sufficiently prepared to go forth as ones prepared - I say ye are as yet not sufficiently prepared to go forth as ye are called - when called - the obedience unto the call is so necessary - most necessary - for this is the device We of the Host hast devised for the ones which have ears to hear - so let them be sharpened and the mind be quickened that ye might know the time and the action to be taken for I say unto thee there shall be action and it is in this manner that ye shall know what action ye shall take - Now I say unto thee Mine Servant whom I have alerted at this hour ye shall give this unto them which are prepared to hear, and to get up and listen for the directions which we will/shall give unto them which are ready to follow our orders for we know that which We are about - So be it that there are many which shall give unto us the "bitter cup" - that matters not unto us - for We are well trained "Commanders" - We fear no man or the sneers of them which sneer neither their foolish tongues - So let them be warned - So be it I have spoken fearlessly and wisely unto One which I have trained well that she might be as one prepared to serve the good of all in the time of need - So be it and Selah.

Champion am I - I go My own stride - I consult no man, moon or tide.

Recorded by
Sister Thedra

ESU SPEAKS FROM THE CHRIST

MY CHILD...the pressures upon you are great, but not beyond your tolerance, for you are a WARRIOR, and behind you, an ARMY advances to VICTORY. You, my child, are as an AVENUE for those who come to make WAY for even GREATER ARMIES OF DESCENT.

How can the battle t'wixt LIGHT and DARK be conducted to a completion, if darkness hides its face behind veils of material masks? Is it not for the WARRIORS to expose these FACTIONS, and this by drawing them out into their nakedness, that the LIGHT can enter their SECRET HIDING PLACES, and lay them to naught?

Do I not have my CALLED? And are they of all one achievement--or are they of _many_ capabilities? Indeed, many are WARRIORS--and even of these, are they of varied ACTIONS of ASSIGNMENT and DETAIL of DUTY. There are those who walk deep in the shadows, pointing out the CREVICES where lie hidden the ones who lurk to stealthily spring upon my LAMBS--and as hidden ravenous wolves-- they must be EXPOSED and disposed of as _threats_ to my PEACE which _must_ come upon EARTH.

There are those of my CALLED who work _openly_ to HERALD the COMING, and who do GREAT WORKS in their _evidences_...yet, even a GREATER WORK, not suspected by those who observe the outer, is performed upon PLANÉS not obvious.

Yes, these weary, as they carry the greater burden--for theirs be the greater _attack_, as they strive in the world of men to bring LIGHT, and strive in the buried kingdoms, to cast a PATH--an avenue--for the ARMIES OF HIS MIGHT to travel upon. For, _is_ it not the CHARGE

31

of those who <u>have</u> a <u>place</u> in KINGDOMS, to <u>invite</u>, and <u>invoke</u> HIS WILL to go forth, and HIS ARMIES to descend?

Need it be said that there are those children of darkness who serve their master in ways of like <u>action</u>--in that they challenge, through their words and deeds, the WORKS and ACTIONS of the CHILDREN OF LIGHT? Are these things difficult for your understanding?

It is NOT the WAY of SPIRIT to do battle--but man creates the IMAGE of WAR--and by his falling away into falsehood, a necessity for HEAVENLY COMPENSATIONS brings forth a RIGHTEOUS IMAGE to challenge <u>his</u> ways.

So it would be, that those who are of EARTH and her sub-planes, who are <u>open</u> to the SPIRIT OF TRUTH, are direct-lines-of-contact from the HIGHER into the LOWER, and are faced by those who challenge from the LOWER. This is why it was said, that families would turn upon their own, for there are those who are in their ignorance, prompted by the OPRESSORS--and who by their lack of WISDOM turn upon those who seek only to bring CHRIST into a darkened world…and even those who seek to do RIGHT, in moments of weakness, can be prevailed upon to REACT in a manner below their <u>aspiration</u>.

It is well that you REALIZE, the end of the struggle nears---and in its final throes, the clash between FORCES is strongly felt by ALL. The greatest struggle of a dying force comes at its final moments.

TRUTH has its edge, and gains in its STRENGTH. The WAR of POWERS and PRINCIPALITIES shall soon subside, and man shall find his PEACE.

CHRIST COMES AS A LIGHT THAT SHINETH AND
DARKNESS SHALL CEASE…!!!

WITH ARMIES OF HEAVEN, and WARRIORS of EARTH

CHRIST SHALL REIGN…!!!

TRANSCRIBED BY TESKA
I AM ESU ---CALLED JESUS

"LITERALLY CITIES WITHIN THE AIR"

Good evening, Tuieta. It is Aleva to continue. As you can feel by the warmth, my energies are quite close to you and quite concentrated. As you write this, you will note that even your handwriting is modified from your usual. Dear sister, there is such joy in our communication with you ones of Earth. I am so honored to be allowed to share with you some of the observations and preparations here. My mentor here is dear Commander Haton for I am under his guidance and tutelage. There is so much that I wish to share with you but your method of communication - your words - cannot begin to describe all that is in our hearts. I shall speak of the ships to familiarize you with them. First and largest are our Mother ships which would be likened to one of your cities such as your capital city, Washington B.C. (excuse me, I believe I am in error, it is supposed to be D.C. Correct?) These are literally cities within the air.

The next size is the Command ships which might be likened to your football field size. Then there are the ships of the sector leaders which are slightly smaller. Then there is a variety of smaller ones down to the remote controlled scout ships. In the time of lift off all will be used to bring you up from Earth as quickly as possible. You will be sorted to the correct Mother ships as you are beamed up. I would add the key to the safe and expedient transition is to have no fear - HAVE NO FEAR. We endeavor in our communiques to alleviate any fear that you might have. As we read the monitors we see many questions that pertain to your present state on Earth now. Some we are unable to answer because they will no longer be pertinent once you have joined us. So many things of earthly consequence now shall be relegated to the pile of trivia in the days to come. So my dear sister, this is the reason for many of man's unanswered questions. (Yes, Tuieta, please share this with <u>ALL</u>.) Many of you are saying that you have not been in our ships. Not so.

During the past five years most of you have spent much of your sleeping hours with us. It is just not time to activate your recall. Indeed when you come onboard you will feel quite at home and quite familiar with your surroundings. Some of you in the days before you may begin to experience brief flashes of these sojourns. This will happen as we begin your activation. I am told my allotted portion is almost over for this hour. Peace to all men of Earth. God's Will shall reign. Good night and thank you, my sister.

Recorded by Tuieta of the Emerald Cross
Ft. Wayne, Indiana

"TO ENGAGE EACH OTHER IN SPIRITUAL CONTACT"

Nov 4th, 1984 -- Received by Harold Harvey, Leduc, Alberta, CANADA

Greetings to you my friends, for we in Space come to you --- we have communicated with you have been in your presence many times. We have shared your love and communication within your sanctuary.

We hover and are ever near you. We have not been able to establish contact with you, for you have not at this time been able to raise up your elevation of vibration to meet with ours to have a common meeting point between the two.

But fear not -- for the time is coming closer and closer whereby we will be able to engage each other in spiritual contact from outer space with you on this earth plane.

Keep reaching up -- reaching and communicating with God and uplifting your level of oneness with God -- and thru this ye shall be able to communicate, for we have much to share with you.

For great changes will happen upon this earth plane, and you must be ready for us. We will communicate and we shall be the ones that will be there in the event of any catastrophe --- for this has been given to us as our purpose, or as a destiny.

Fear not, for we come in love, we come in humility and we come in oneness with mankind. For we have been near the earth plane for eons of time -- we have been the ones who have guided mankind to better and better things upon this earth plane.

Again, there are the ones that abuse the knowledge of Christ, they abuse the knowledge of science and of man and of those things that have been given to mankind to utilize and to use.

There must be a reckoning -- and it is only thru our communication with you that we shall be able to establish our time tables or changes, and the time that we may be one with you so that we can communicate with you when the time is near. A way shall be found.

Fear not! -- for ye have been chosen to be watched over and be guided. Ye shall be lifted up - ye shall be taken away from this -- ye shall return at a later date, when all things shall be ready.

God Bless Ye! ---- for we are near you. - Ye shall be notified. There shall come a time again when ye shall see us, ye shall see us in our craft -- in our space craft. This shall be known to you -- this shall be our communication to let you know that we are here.

So fear not -- for as long as there is harmony and love, we come.

>God Bless You!
>Be open and ready -- for we are near.
>God Bless You.

the formality will be dispensed with because of the large numbers we shall be working with in a relatively short period of time. I am told that I shall close for this hour and I hope it is the will of the Divine One, our Lord Sananda, I shall speak with you again. Good night, my dear brothers and sisters, good night.

Received thru Tuieta of the Emerald Cross
Ft. Wayne, Indiana

MYSTERIOUS WAYS?

Be ye as ones prepared for a great part. For as the winds doth blow, and the storms doth come, and the rivers doth rise, and the snow doth come - so doth the Sun shine, and so doth the roses bloom, and so doth the Hand of God move in mysterious ways.

I say: Mysterious ways? Yet do I not know the movement thereof.

I say unto thee: I know the movement of the Hand of God. And too, I see the handwriting on the wall.

I KNOW the meaning thereof.

Let it be said that One shall stand before thee and declare the Word, and He shall be as one which hast been given the fullness of its meaning - for He shall be as One quickened - and yet He shall be as one despised and shunned by men. He shall be as one which knows the meaning of suffering and sorrow, for this hast been His lot.

I say: "This hast been his lot".

Ye shall be as ones prepared, for He shall show thee many things.

So be it and Selah

Recorded by
Sister Thedra

FOR LONG HAVE THEY BEEN FOREWARNED

Sori Sori - The hour draweth nigh when ye shall be brought forth as one prepared - ye shall stand as one prepared for I have set Mine Seal upon thee and it is given unto Me to know Mine Own - So be it and Selah.

Sori Sori - Like unto the water which roll upon the shores shall the people be tossed about and they shall run to and from crying for help yet I say they shall find none, for long have they been forewarned - It is now come when great shall be their stress and their suffering shall be as nothing they have known - It is the will of the Father that they be prepared for that which is nigh upon the -- Yet when they heed not the warning they shall be responsible for their own suffering - for We of the Host call out unto them "Come, Come forth" and they move not - I say they are as ones dead - they hear not neither do they look or see -

Let it be said that they shall be as ones which have betrayed themself - let them be for it is given unto thee to have a divine part to play and ye shall be responsible for thine own part - So be it and Selah.

"QUESTIONS CONCERNING THE SHIPS"

Truieta: Aleva states that she has been given the opportunity to answer some questions if we have some questions concerning the ships. And she assures you there are things about the ships that she doesn't know but she would be quite happy to share what she does know with us.

Question: The great room that she spoke of, is there only one of these on the ship where everybody will be going or are there several?

Aleva: There is one great room that we will all be going to as we come into the ships. Now in her haste and her enthusiasm she didn't describe this room and she says - it is a large reception hall that all will be gathering in but in my haste, in my enthusiasm, I did not share with you amphitheater which we have where there will be meetings conducted. There are also small, smaller, anterooms off the main reception hall where groups might also gather. But initially there shall be one great room where those of the celestial hierarchy and those of us of the Confederation and those of you of Earth might gather initially to ease your transition into our dimension. Now here I speak of the reception room on the mother ships. Some of you shall be coming up to smaller ships initially to be beamed to the mother ships, the command ships later. Now this later is a very short time I assure you. In Earth terms it could be but a matter of moments, less than one hour of your earth time.

Question: Could you tell us some more about the role of the children that Commander Haton talked of?

Aleva: You of Earth gaze upon children as the precious gifts that are given to your charge for a time. You see them grow into adulthood, to assume their role upon the earthly plane. Here we see the children in a different light for we see the soul that is housed within this being and its total of experiences, its knowledge, its acquired wisdom, that soul that has evolved along its path. Our children shall come forth in their true maturity, and here I shall speak of soul maturity, for many of them have come forth on your plane at this time merely to hasten their transition between the two planes. Now there shall be ones that shall appear as children but these are the young souls that have not evolved to the degree that others have, indeed they are children in the journey of their soul. Does that help, my brother?

Question: The ones we will meet in the great room, will some of them be our earthly relatives, friends that have passed on, our earthly acquaintances as well as our soul acquaintances?

Aleva: Yes, yes, yes, yes, yes, yes and won't it be joyful for we shall all be together and we shall recognize one another and we shall all embrace in the universal and how joyous it will be! I would urge you to do all within your capability within your present dimension to raise your vibratory rate for this shall hasten your transition with us and make it easier for you. My dear brothers and sisters we are on the final countdown and such joy we have awaiting your arrival. When the hour comes it shan't be necessary for you to bring any of your would-be clothing with you. All that you need will be provided. All that you shall require will be in your room. Do not be concerned about taking anything with you. Because this will be an evacuation phase much of the formality will be dispensed with because of the large numbers we shall be working with in a relatively short period of time. I am told that I shall close for this hour and I hope it is the will of the Divine One, our Lord Sananda. I shall speak with you again. Good night, my dear brothers and sisters, good night.

Received thru Tuleta

Of the Emerald Cross

Ft. Wayne, Indiana

"WE COME SOLELY BECAUSE OF OUR LOVE"

Beloved Ones: The offer of sight is the Promise given, and it is thine when thou art prepared to receive it.

I say unto thee: Thine eyes could not endure the Glory of God; thine eyes could not behold it, go great is His Glory. I speak unto thee of Light which thou knowest not of, for such Light thou hast not seen.

Let it be said, that there is none which could endure the grandeur of His Presence; for this does it become necessary to dim thine eyes, that ye see but faintly, and thru a veil darkly - yet the veil shall be removed in time, and so great shall be thy joy, that ye shall be as ones transfixed, and thine being shall be filled with joy. And then ye shall turn to give unto thine faltering brothers a hand, even as We, thine Older Brothers have given Ours, that ye be lifted up.

So be it that We come solely because of Our Love and compassion for thee. Thine unknowing is a pitiful plight, and for this hast it been of Our own will that We offer our assistance, that ye too might come to know such joy - let it be, for We of the Mighty Host shall be as the Host; We shall be as the ones which shall sing out with great Joy, when thou hast been liberated from bondage, and for this do We wait.

Be ye blest of Me and by Me, for I am come that ye be blest - so let it be.

I AM Sananda

Recorded by
Sister Thedra

43

A GREAT ASSEMBLAGE OF LIGHTED ONES

I am Monka to speak and again my dear ones, my message shall be brief. There is currently within our realms a great assemblage of Lighted ones of all the universes and galaxies. These ones are here to be closer to you, our brothers and sisters, in these hours, and to offer assistance to stay dear Mother Earth for a few more hours, or to assist in her evacuation should our other efforts be of no avail. As you go forth from this dwelling and gaze upon the stars, know that many many more than your eye can see are also represented and involved for you and with you. As you turn your thoughts to us we feel of your love and sharing, and are warmed in your faithfulness with us. Dear ones, I would urge you that in the ensuing time look not to world or elemental happenings as catastrophes. Greet each in light and know it is of purpose, know that each act has come forth, no matter how large or small, as a direct result of mans own actions. Balance shall be, harmony shall be. Man, this mortal man, shall not alter the Plan for all of creation. What our Father has created, let no man put asunder, for by his hand man shall be accountable. Peace be with you, may love from our Radiant One fill your hearts to overflowing. We of the Intergalactic Fleet salute you and stand ever ready to assist you. I am your brother signing off.

Received thru: Tuieta of the Golden Cross

THE CONDITION OF THE HEART

Oct 18, 1984

Judge ye not thy neighbor nor the life conditions of another for I say I have collected Light from the Arms of the Father and the Breast of The Mother. I have collected Light - that most precious gift of Life and I have come quietly with My arms full. I have come silently in the night and I have planted.

While My sheep have slumbered I have looked to the condition of their hearts.

I have seen those who's hearts were cold and stony and I have passed them by for until this condition is alleviated by the owner, no thing of Light will flourish there and I am not one to waste My precious cargo. And so I have passed that one by and yet I did embrace that one, for love that one I do and yet I have moved on for it is The Law that that child is responsible for the condition of the heart and so I move on to the next.

I see possibility here. True the field is rocky and yet I do see some fertile places -- And so I plant the seeds of Light between the rock and I fertilize the soil there with Mine own tears. I weep for the pain the rocky places have brought. I weep for the heaviness they cause. I pray they will not corrupt the growth of Light here. I bless this one and I move on to the next.

Now here I find a field already prepared and tilled. The soil here is rich and fertile, ready for My hand and so place the seeds of Antrum one by one into the heart prepared. This time My tears are born of Joy for I see there is no foreign thing here to block out the Ray from The Central Sun.

Again I say judge ye not for I say your vision is one born of opinions. Too often you judge another by what you see and I say too often you see only the smallest corner of the whole picture. Very often the most lighted of My flock are placed in very dark places indeed -- And I say when the time comes I shall activate that which I have planted and at that time all will know where The Light really is. Until then I have asked those with the Golden Hearts to keep quiet - to move dutifully on through their life condition. To be faithful to their agreement with Me and to perform that portion of My work given them to do.

Again I say judge ye not. Do not waste energies allotted foolishly. Instead use that energy to check the condition of your heart -- AND BE HONEST WITH YOURSELF! Do you fill your mind with cold negative Thoughts? Do you concentrate on pain, sorrow and grief? Do you consciously act IN Love or do you use "love" as a tool to have your own way? These are some of the conditions of the cold and stony heart and Light will not exist without warmth. You and you alone are responsible for the condition of your heart and ultimately you will be the judge of that condition.

If you long to come to the Grande Feast waiting to celebrate the rebirthing of Mother Earth, you had best clear the stone from your heart, warm it up and prepare the field for planting NOW - for I say with authority -- this is the last planting for comes the winter soon and this winter will be like no other before it and only the warmth of a Lighted heart will be your savior. To those who survive I say the spring follows the trials of the winter and that spring will be like no other before it. On golden meadows, fragrant and warm will wait a banquet and that feast shall be like no other before it.

I will meet you there on the other side of the mountain.

I Am your Elder Brother

Sananda

Received by Kai King
P.O. Box 3436, Gardena, CA 90249

"THE ACTION WHICH IS NOW BEING TAKEN"

By what hand shall they be spared? By what hand shall they be brought out? By what Power? By what Authority?

I ask of them: By what hand hast thou been sustained? By whose Grace has thou been spared - by whose Wisdom?

Now let it be said: Were it not for the wisdom which is endowed unto Us of the Father, thou wouldst not endure, thou wouldst not be able to breathe, for it is by the consolidated efforts of the Great and Mighty Host, and the Grand Council, that the action hast been taken which shall become apparent unto thee -- unto the dense ones - unto them which yet sleepeth!

I say: The action which is now being taken, shall become apparent unto each and every one which has one iota of comprehension.

I too say that: We are not so foolish as to fall asleep, for there is much to be done. Let it be said, that at no time in man's history hast he been able to bear witness of such action, as is now taking place within the realms of Light, and within the realms of the seen; for the action of which I speak, shall be seen and felt within the world of man - yet I say:

They have not seen such as they shall see, for it shall be unlike any other action which has hitherto been enacted upon the Earth! I say: Man hast not witnessed that which he shall witness, for he has not been aware of that which hast first taken place on the planes just above that of the material world - the place in which he now functions, and which he is aware of. For this do We say: "Be ye aware of that which goes on about thee, and many things shall be revealed unto thee". So be it I

48

speak out for the sake of all which have a mind to hear Me - so let them hear, for none other shall hear.

I am with thee that they be alerted.

So be it I AM Sananda

Recorded by
Sister Thedra

I AM COME THAT IT CEASE

This day let it be understood that the way has been made clear that ye might return unto thine rightful estate - thine abiding place it is given unto Me to make straight the way - and for this am I called the "Way Shower" for this do I say: "follow ye Me that where I go ye might go also" and it shall be for thine own enlightenment that I give unto thee this word that there are a great many which have come with Me that the way be prepared before thee - It is given unto us the 'host' to see that which goes on, and that which is being done - yet we stand by in readiness to be unto thee the hand and foot so swift that no man could follow in its flight - the time is come when naught shall stay us - for the time is come when great stress is upon the land and the people thereof has within their hand the power to set into motion that which could destroy the Earth, and at no time shall We allow that - for this it is given unto Us the power and the authority to stop that which has been brought about by their own willfulness - and wanton - I say the time is come when we shall interfere with the plan of men!!

For they have gone so far as to give unto the Earth the bitter cup - which shall be unto Her, Her destruction without our help - so shall it be assured Her, that She shall not perish at the hands of the dragon!!

I have set Mine hand against them and they shall know that it is so - so shall it be -

While they dare call themself "civilized and christian" I say they have not known the meaning of ethic - they are not of Mine fold - so be it that I am about Mine Fathers business and I fear naught - and I say unto them make way! for I am at the helm - and I pass and they shall stand in awe, and know that I have past - so be it I shall pass them by - and they shall cry out for assistance and I shall not hear their cry for they have set their foot against Me and betrayed themself - so be it I have spoken out against the war mongers and the ones which set brother against brother - and son against father - mother against daughter and sister against brother -

I say I speak out against them which set one against the other that they might set their foot upon their necks - let it be said that it shall cease - Let it cease!

The Word which hast gone out of Mine mouth shall not return unto Me void - So be it I am come that it cease!

I Am the Lord Thy God

Sananda

Recorded by
Sister Thedra

MAHERU

While it is the time of great stress within the Earth, it is great within the peoples thereof - for they are of the Earth - earthly forms and substance they have, and they separate themself not from the substance of which their bodily forms are composed; they are part of that which composes the body of the blessed Virgo - wherein has She been spared the suffering?

I say: She too is tormented by the dross, the effluvia which the laggards are want to bring, and leave. Too I say that: It shall be given unto the remnant to clean away the dross, and help prepare the Earth for Her new place, Her new part which she so richly deserves - for this was She created.

It is with great compassion that we have come to assist in this, the time of Her cleansing - yet We are not alone in this; many walk amongst thee for that purpose, and these walk for the most part unknown, unsung, unheralded, unannounced, and unveiled - while We are within the Secret places, prepared to assist them in the unveiling.

We go not out amongst them, for there is no necessity for this, when We can best serve Our part from Our places of abode - while it is given unto Our Blessed Lord Sananda, to walk in the midst of them at will. He has taken upon Himself the preponderous task of awakening them which sleep; this is the task of One which hast attained unto "God-Hood"' for this has He been raised unto His present station. While I, Muru/Maheru, have but attained unto the station of a lesser degree, it is Mine part to assist Him in His efforts - the Great Awakening!

When this part is finished, accomplished, I shall present Myself before the Mighty Council, for the next part - then I shall take upon Myself greater responsibility, and I shall receive another appointment - by the consent of the Council. It is My only desire, to serve in the Great Plan, and for the good of all - "ALL" - everywhere, THE ALL.

So may it be that this day be brought to its conclusion in a blaze of Glory, wherein all might be gathered up with Him, the King of Glory. So be it I am come, offering My assistance at this time, for the sake of Mine Brothers, which are yet asleep - they shall awaken, and follow where He leads them.

Many shall find themself without shelter, food or clothing - yet they shall become aware of their Source, and they shall be glad for it shall be given unto them to know they are not alone.

So be it I shall speak into thee again this day.

I AM Meheru

Recorded by
Sister Thedra
School of the Seven Rays

LESSONS IN "LIGHT" LIVING: PART IX

THE ANIMALS

"If you can sip of the Essence of Love, and can experience its fullness and richness, you will know its depth, its height and its breadth. Your love will know no bounds, nor be limited by any inhibitions or blockages. In fact, it will encompass all of Creation. For the human being, this usually means that it encompasses all of that portion of Creation of which he is aware: his own fellow-beings, the whole of the Animal Kingdom, the Plant or Vegetable Kingdom and the Mineral Kingdom. If you have sipped of the Essence of Love you will know that ALL IS, and you are a part of the ALL, and the ALL is part of you.

Just think of how your race has so cruelly treated these innocent, helpless and often beautiful creatures. How man has exploited, murdered, poisoned, maimed and deformed them; all in his own selfish pursuits...

In one sense, it was not intended that animals should be 'wild' although it was the Creator's intention that these animals should live in their natural habitats - not subject to interference in their way of living by man. Nevertheless, they were to be the <u>friends</u> of man, and <u>co-workers with man</u>, upon your Planet."

ANIMAL RAPPORT

"It has been said that animals who live closely with man and are domesticated, or semi-domesticated, have psychic powers and are able to communicate telepathically with their masters and mistresses. It is true that animals brought up within the influence of a human aura can learn much of their master or mistress from comprehension and appreciation of the moods which show themselves within the auric field. An animal is quick to pick up the mood of a human being... of fear, anger, restlessness, gentleness, pity and love.

It is living within the proximity of the human aura that enables the animal to evolve to a Higher Level, partly through an expansion of its own language and ways and means of conveying to the human mind...its desires or intentions; also the fact that, through understanding and experimenting within the environs of the human aura, they learn to understand man. You can see that in this way they are aided in their evolution to a more intelligent life in a later Life-stream."

ANIMALS AS HEALERS

"This channel received a hint concerning the use of animals in healing. There is nothing sensational in this! We were referring to the fact that animals may be used by man, or the animals themselves will instinctively behave in such a way, so that they are able to bring love and comfort to human beings in distress of mind, emotional-instability or great sorrow. An animal by its presence, when it is sensitive enough (and in this case, of course, this refers mainly to domestic animals who are closely associated with man), can convey, by its behaviour, sympathy and companionship for the lonely - for animals, too, can be lonely, as are many human beings.

One other aspect we would like you to turn your attention to - an important aspect, from Our viewpoint - which We think you will acknowledge is of equal importance; and that is the example set by animals before mankind (domestic or wild, but particularly in their wild state) and especially decadent man in his crumbling society. For animals in their natural environment exercise and manifest many of those virtues which, at your best, you uphold and revere. Need we enumerate these? You are aware of the painstaking dexterity with which an animal will build its habitat. How a beaver or an otter will move two and fro gathering driftwood, weeds and various pieces of debris, natural foliage and twigs, just as a bird will build its dwelling - and, that being swept away, he will commence all over again. You have many examples of patience, perseverance, fortitude, hard work, courage or self-sacrifice - for animals will starve rather than see their young die of hunger before their eyes. They can be fearless; they can be devoted parents; and, in their old age, can show a strange stoicism."

FARM ANIMALS - AURIC FIELDS OF ANIMALS

"If you walk in a field among a herd of cattle or a flock of sheep are you not impressed by the quietude, the calm and harmony of that atmosphere amidst the beauties of Nature? ...and also influenced, in part, by these gentle animals who are content and for periods of time know no fear? You are experiencing their mass auric field! For they, too, are ensouled and radiate that calm and peace which has a healing influence upon the weary and tortured minds of men. This is why the shepherds and other keepers of animals were men of peace, who had a philosophy of life and were imbued with the gentleness of the animals they cared for.

So we say to you - those of you who are fortunate enough to live away from the cities - spare a few hours to walk the countryside and savour this atmosphere which is as balm to the soul by calming troubled minds. You cannot live in the chaos of city life without it having an adverse effect upon you."

MAN, THE GUARDIAN OF ANIMALS'

"Beloved children, in the beginning upon this Planet man walked with God - and His Angels and Beings of Light; and in their turn, the Lesser Kingdom, the Animals and Birds, walked and talked with men. For, in those days, they understood one another and all was loving trust, harmony and obedience.

Then the time came when man chose to think differently, and to behave in ways which were not the Father's Ways. Changes began to take place upon your Planet which have lasted to this day, for the balance of Nature was disturbed. As man in his blindness and willfulness has altered so much on your Planet, and has destroyed or upset the Natural Equilibrium of Life in its Lower Forms, so they have reacted upon the Animals, and the relationship with the Animal Kingdom is no longer as it was intended to be. For many centuries Man has shown a callous disregard for those who were placed into his care, as his friends and companions, to evolve together.

Man knows how he can influence others and how he should set an example to his own children. Are not the animals of Earth also his children? - insofar as they have been loaned to man and placed in his custody. He has set a bad example to these 'lesser brethren' his 'children', and they have grown to mistrust and hate him, to fear his activities, for he has betrayed his trust, and has ill-treated them to 'amuse' himself and his companions. (We refer to cock-fighting, bear-baiting, otter- and fox-hunting, bullfights and man activities which take place in the countryside, the back streets, the inner-rooms of drug-infested places, and also among those who practice the 'black arts' where animal sacrifice is often carried out.) Need we refer to the work of the laboratories and the scientific institutions?... Few animals there are which do not cringe at the sound of the footsteps of men,

Man ceased to eat the fruits, herbs and seeds only of the Earth. He set a bad example when he ate flesh; and some animals, seeing this, became flesh-eaters also. It was not always so! - for in the Father's Creation all is perfect balance, order and harmony. Cruelty should not exist...either between Animal and Animal, Animal and Man, or Man and Animal.

Beloveds, it is only in the remote and holy places of your world, where all living things are reverenced, loved and respected, that the animals are safe, where they live UN-molested, and regard man as a friend. There is a telepathic rapport between, with no intent to harm each other, for the Holy Man blesses them, and they come to sit at his feet in peace.

If you look at the chaotic conditions in Nature you will realize that that TIME is very near when changes must be made to preserve what is left of the Creation indigenous to this planet. There is so much beauty which you have cast aside. You have lost all interest in it for you have become so obsessed and absorbed in manmade creations, having discarded the bountiful beauties of Nature and the lessons and joys to be gained from them.

When man has learned to walk the Earth without weapons...with hands outstretched...then shall the animals respond to him again, without fear, to enjoy a wonderful and mutual rapport of companionship, freedom and respect. PUT DOWN YOUR WEAPONS, MEN OF EARTH! Put down your sticks and stones! Unclench your fists and relax...and permit the animals to relax with you! For when there is order on this Planet there will be Beauty again, and Peace and Understanding. When your hands are no longer stained with the blood of your own Brothers and the Lesser-Brethren, THEN shall Harmony be restored.

Animals were not created for exploitation, nor to be used in war, or peace! - to suffer and die. Their Brethren on the Higher Planes are aware of this suffering and know that Man must repay ALL before he can enter the Kingdom of Light. This Law must always prevail - for this is the Justice of the Father Mother God. Insofar as you are loving and merciful to animals, birds and other creatures, so shall Divinity be merciful to you."

DEBTS TO ANIMALS

"Recurring dreams of lacerations, tortures, confinements and restrictions while on the Astral Planes (during sleep) are a just 'retribution' for the torments Man has inflicted throughout the centuries upon dumb creatures, both wild and domestic. You have looked upon them with scorn, ever fear, and you have exploited them in unforgiveable ways, for they are totally and ultimately defenseless against your whiles, your traps and gins, your guns and laboratories of scientific research.

How can animals live at peace with their fellow creatures in the New Dispensation if they still fear men? You have to work to remove this deep fear and make full restitution for your crimes."

"This is Man's most disasterous folly - the willful exploitation for pleasure or profit of this Kingdom, especially the animals which feel pain and thus build up great fear-patterns on the Planet. The vandalism of the Earth by ruthless and selfish men demands Karmic Retribution.

This, of course, is where Light Workers must themselves accept the Karma of Mankind upon their shoulders; for these brothers who carry out these terrible cruelties are but infants in their spiritual evolution. "Forgive them, Lord, for they know not what they do!" The Christed One said this when they killed him; and when they kill the younger brethren, the animals, they still do not realize what they do.

This is where your earthly organizations against blood sports, vivisection etc. are working for the Light. They are bringing these cruelties to the notice of mankind that they may be banned. This is good and necessary. When will man's karma towards the animals be lifted? When he stops misusing his brethren and loves them; takes them into his arms and carries them forward in their evolution."

With regard to the Coming Changes, it seems to us we should reassure you that the domestic animals of a loving disposition, positively orientated, are protected within the auric field of their owners.

Do not think because the Earth is to be changed you will be divorced from the Animal Kingdom. For upon the New Earth there will be new creatures, great and small. Those domestic animals close to human beings will be preserved and be with them.

Man's responsibility extends to the Vegetable and Mineral Kingdoms also, it is because of his greed and ignorance that they are in a state of chronic imbalance.

The Devic kingdoms and the Kingdoms of Nature - the fairies, elves and so on are also deeply affected and disturbed by the exploitation of their kingdoms. The elements themselves have been upset by man's behaviour and are now in a state bordering on revolt.

Man bears responsibility for the chaotic situation in all areas and for the sick condition of the Planet herself. By realizing the ONENESS and therefore the inter-relatedness of all Life and by the application of the Law of Love of Harmlessness, man can begin to create conditions in which the true Plan of God will manifest."

Angels Speak

Oct. 15, 1984

Forgive them Father for they know not what they do.

Lord, they have come again, many with no requirement to come again and yet their heart was tender to Earth and Her children. They have volunteered to come again to serve in Love. And yet, tho they were free of the boundaries of Earth and heavy atmospheres, for they had earned their Light Bodies, they said yes to the call to arms - for the sake of Earth and Her inhabitants. So they came again through the process of birth through the womb of woman.

O Beloved Father, Perfect Mother, in Thy Graciousness and by Thy Love, We ask forgiveness for those who with pure intention entered the heavy atmosphere of Tara and due to the exposure of Earthly karma and the siren call of the serpent have fallen and crushed their wings - and they now lie in confusion and have lost their knowing.

Beloved Father, Perfect Mother if it is Thy Will, We shall put Our Wings of Light beneath, to cushion their fall. We will put Our Arms about them to hold them once again steady. And if Thou wouldst will it so, We, The Commanders of Light will lift them back to the "hospital" where they can be cleansed and healed from their "accident".

Lord of All, We ask Thy Blessings for these ones. We know that the intention of the heart is recorded as well as the accomplishments of each soul. In recognition of this fact, We, Thy first Born ask forgiveness upon these ones who have erred. In the fullness of Thy Love We bask and warm Ourselves knowing All is well by Thy Design.

We are Sananda, Ashtar, Athena, Zoe, Korton, Allana, Osiris, Merian, Urial, Iriahl, Gabriel, Tita-tching-ghung-goi, and Kwan Yin.

The Son (Sun) Brings Word

I come from the Temple of Wholeness and Oneness. I have sat quiet before The Throne of our Lord God The Most High. I have breathed in The Essence of Life. I have listened while My Father spoke and now I come to give unto thee The Word as it was given unto Me; the first Born, the first Son - Sun, The Flame of The Christ Light.

I say I have sat quiet before The Throne where My Mother hast gazed upon Me with eyes of Love as I correctly and precisely recorded The Word of My Father.

This is The Word:

I am Creator. I have created the Heavens and the Earth. I have molded each star with Mine Own Hand and I have infused each star with Mine Own Light.

Now I wish to speak to those who will believe that their Father does speak.

I say I have not stilled My Voice. NO!

I have given My Mighty and Wonderful Bible to man and man read of My Word and then promptly put his fingers in his ears.

62

I say I go on! I do <u>not</u> give one final word and then cease to speak. Nor do I create once and cease to develop new life and to create new horizons. I have said it before and I will say it again; I Am The Alpha and The Omega; I Am forever and for <u>All</u> Ways!

I say man attempts to squeeze God into a small form that he can understand. This <u>cannot</u> be done. In days of old when man was young he thought God was a rock - and he carved that rock into his likeness and he called that God and he worshiped that rock. Yes - that rock is of Me - and yet that rock is not Me. As man grew he came to view a star or a sun as God. He grew and then came to view the heavens as God. And I say the stars and the suns are of Me and yet they are not Me.

So man knew a portion and as he grew he came to know a greater portion. He knew a portion of My Wholeness and yet he knew not of My Fullness. Now Man has grown much since his birth onto Earth and yet even now he seeks to mold and carve and stuff God into the little space he calls his brain. I say, man, you cannot intellectualize God. Only your heart can know the greater part -- and even your heart can only know a part. Man is also inclined to want to dissect and analyze what is commonly known as God ---- And he does this very thing with My Holy Books.

He pours over them - criticizes what he does not understand or what is unappealing to him never understanding the fullness of My Word or the true meaning there-of -- Nor the pure language contained in the Messages.

O Beloved Man of Earth do you seek The Light? Do you seek union with your Creator? - Then stop taking pieces of God and calling it the whole.

Now let Me continue for this day I long to educate you in matters vital to your survival.

You like to think of flesh as the primary reality. -- Not so! It is the spirit that is of The Ever Lasting Life.

You have come to the moment in your evolution where you have and do explore other planets and in your limited understanding you pompously declare that other planets are lifeless. "The climate is too thin or too hot or too cold to support life as we know it" you say. And man, in your arrogance you believe these planets you have viewed, with your clouded vision, are beneath you on the evolutionary scale. True some are -- and yet these are very few in this universe. Have I not said I have molded each star and every sun with Mine Own Hand -- And did I not say too that I have infused each with Mine Own Light? Listen to Me well "Where there is Light there is Life." How can you expect to see the life in The Light when you do not even recognize the light in your brothers on Earth?

I say you see not -- you hear not -- you know not. I say with Mine Own Authority there are Grand Cities on High that you see not and they are peopled by souls far advanced from that of man in ways of technology, from intellect as well as spirituality. I say too that these benevolent Ones are responsible for mans continued existence on Earth. More times than I will say the Beloved Brothers of Pure Form have rescued man from his own folly - And I say They, the Beloved Ones of Whole Light come again to give of Themselves to alleviate the condition man has created of or himself.

Listen to Me NOW - for soon comes the cleansing and once begun all those who have refused to hear Me and Mine will perish - to sleep - and then once again to "climb the steep mountain" - to continue to know pain and disease and confusion - and to once again struggle unknowing toward that portion of self that is of God.

Is this how you would design your future? Or will you open your ear to My Call and will you open your heart and let Me fill up all the lonely spaces?

Hear Me now when I say there are changes of great and unthought-of magnitude coming -- and come they must for Mother Earth is overdue and it is Her right to move forward in the Heavens. Comes Her time <u>soon</u> and when Her time is upon Her there will be great upheavals of pain and the land masses will shift and the waters shall abide where large cities once stood and man will find no secure place to put his foot.

Now listen to this; I have given My Angels and My Children of Whole Light charge over thee. At the moment of the Great Birthing the skies will fill with ships. It is the purpose of these ships to rescue those who have developed their love vibration sufficiently to be boarded. Also the children will be taken aboard in the first sweep.

None other shall be rescued in this manner. Crying and wailing and pleading will not be a boarding pass to those who do not qualify. Even with the skies full of rescue ships there will be some who will sacrifice their flesh body to stay as long as possible to assist those who in the last moments will quickly come to understanding. Upon passing from the pore (flesh) the spirit of these ones - along with those they have "rescued, : will be surrounded by Legions of Angels. The trumpets will sound and rainbows will shower the Earth, as those who gave so much will be escorted to The Holy of Holies to receive their reward.

This is My Word this day. I have spoken.

Go My Beloved Son - Sun - Go and tell My people. Give unto them exactly as I have given unto You. Go swiftly for the clock will stand still for no man. I have spoken and it be so. They must be ready now and they must stay ready for the day of reckoning will come when no man expects it. Stay alert!

And so I Sananda, The Light of the world, deliver into the hand of Mine servant Kai King, The Word of The Lord Our Most Holy and Perfect Father Mother, Creator. I say this Mine servant is trustworthy to deliver The Word Pure.

Received on Oct. 16 and 17, 1984
By Kai King, P.O. Box 3436, Gardena, CA 90247

"FATHER, OH BLESSED FATHER"

Most Holy and Perfect Father - Giver and Taker of Life - for Thou art the ALL:

O' Father of Us all: Be it so that these Thine Sons become aware of the fullness of their inheritance - their Light which is Thine, which is endowed them thru and by Thine Grace.

I speak unto Thee Father, that they might come to know that they are Thine Sons, with the power and the authority to speak unto Thee as I have - that Thou hearest them, even as Thou hast heard Me. Cause them to hear Me, that they might come to know Thee as I know Thee.

Father, Oh Blessed Father: I come before them in supplication, that their hearts might be softened, that they might be quickened and know that thou hast heard, Father, for Thine Mercy this hast been made possible - yet they know only in part; yet they know not the fullness of Thine Love - that which Thou hast given unto them as their inheritance.

Be it so Father, that they are Thine Sons which sleep within flesh. I say unto them: AWAKEN! - and Mine Word hast gone out from Mine mouth: LET THEM AWAKEN! and become ALIVE! and know that there is a place prepared for them, and that they have a time and a place. Let the time of sleep be finished, and the time of awakening be this day, that they might return unto Thee with Me. So be it Father, that We Thine Sons, sent that they be brought, shall await the Great Day of Awakening! So be it a great day of rejoicing.

Let it be as Thou hast willed. All Praise unto Thee, and all the Glory is Thine, Father - so shall it ever be, worlds without end.

I AM Thine Son
Sananda

Recorded by Sister Thedra
of the Emerald Cross

* * * * * * * *

A CALL TO ARMS

VOL. # 5 ** MESSAGES THRU THE A.S.S.K, GATEHOUSE **1984

THE EARTH'S PATHWAY

Sori Sori -- For this day let it be said: There but ONE God, The Father, and HE hast the power and authority to bring thee out of bondage - yet it is by thine own will that ye are delivered.

Therefore I say unto thee: Be ye as one blest to be as one delivered, for it is now come when ye shall walk as one unbound; as one free from the gravitation; and free from the attraction of the Moon. And at no time shall ye fail, for it is so ordered that ye be brought out of bondage.

The Earth now passes Her Initiation into the pathway which hast been cleared for Her, and She shall endure. And no man shall say unto Me, nay! for it is for this that We of the Mighty Host hast stood by as ones prepared to lift Her up; to bring Her into Her New Place, wherein She shall be made new.

The hour strikes when the Earth and Her children shall be no more bound in darkness. I say, the dawn is come - yet unto thee, I say, ye see not the Light, for it is as though ye were looking thru a dark glass - while the darkness shall pass, and ye shall see clearly within the allotted time. I say, there is a season of sowing and reaping; a season of gladness; a season of joy and sadness; a season of portions; a season of notions; a season of water; a season of drought; a season of knowing; a season of doubt.

Now ye shall go forth as a sower goes forth to his labor. Ye shall be as one prepared, for the season is upon thee when many seed shall fall upon prepared soil, and they shall be nursed, nourished, and they shall come into maturity, and they shall find their mark - they shall do that which was intended from the beginning.

Thus it is that I say, "Be ye as one prepared for a greater part". So be it I shall speak again and again, and ye shall hear Me - so be it and Selah.

Recorded by
Sister Thedra